© Percy Trezise and Dick Roughsey 1978
First published 1978 by William Collins Publishers Pty Ltd, Sydney
Reprinted 1979 (twice)
First published in paperback 1980
Reprinted 1984, 1985, 1988
ISBN 0 00 184370 2 (Hardback)
ISBN 0 7322 7251 3 (Paperback)
Typeset by Dalley Photocomposition, Sydney
Printed by Mandarin Offset, Hong Kong

National Library of Australia
Cataloguing in Publication data
Trezise, Percy J.
The quinkins
For children
I. Roughsey, Dick, joint author. II. Title
A823'.3

PERCY TREZISE and DICK ROUGHSEY

The Quinkins

COLLINS
PUBLISHERS
AUSTRALIA

From the beginning the Yalanji tribe belonged to the
beautiful country of Cape York. They covered the walls
of open caves with their paintings of ancestral beings,
sacred animals—and the Quinkins.

The Quinkins, spirit people of this land, never allowed themselves to be seen by the Yalanji tribe. Yet it was known that there were two groups of Quinkins: the Imjim and the Timara.

The Imjim were small, fat-bellied, bad fellows, with large
ugly heads, long teeth and claws. They stole children and
took them to their cave in the great red mountain called
Boonbalbee. The Imjim had long, knobbly tails that they used
like a kangaroo to travel in giant leaps across the land.

Timara was the name of the other Quinkins. They were humorous, whimsical spirits who liked to play tricks on people, but they didn't like the Imjim stealing children and always tried to stop them. The Timara were very tall—almost as tall as the trees— and so skinny that they lived in the cracks of the rocks.

In an open cave on Lellita Creek lived Moonbi with his
sister Leealin, and their mother Margara and father
Warrenby, also their grandmother.

One afternoon, when their parents were out hunting, Moonbi
and Leealin thought they heard their father calling from far
off in the bush, so they ran to meet him.

It was not their father but an Imjim imitating his voice
to lure the children away to his dark cave in Boonbalbee
mountain where other Imjim waited to turn Moonbi and
Leealin into nasty, ugly creatures like themselves.

The Imjim kept well ahead of the children so that they would not see him. Then he would leap back on his knobbed tail to brush out their tracks so no one could follow. But two willy-wagtails were watching him—so was a Timara Quinkin.

The children met some Yalanji men returning to camp
after their day's hunting.
Moonbi asked, 'Have you seen Warrenby, our father?'

One hunter pointed towards the great red mountain, Boonbalbee, and said he had heard him calling the children from that direction. No one suspected that an Imjim was up to his old tricks.

The children walked on towards Boonbalbee still hearing
their father's voice. Suddenly a large brown snake,
Taipan, reared up in front of them.

Moonbi cried, 'Look out!' and pulled Leealin away before
Taipan could strike her. Hiding nearby, and ready to
help the children, was the Timara.

The children were hungry with all their walking. When they came to a lagoon Moonbi caught a tortoise while Leealin gathered waterlily bulbs and nonda fruit. They made a fire with fire-sticks to cook their food. The Imjim was hungry too. He caught some of his favourite food, large green frogs, to eat.

All this time the Timara was watching, he wanted to rescue
the children. The Timara stretched out his long thin finger
and poked the Imjim in the ribs, giving him such a fright
that he leapt high away over the trees.

Grandmother told Warrenby and Margara that their children
had run off to meet their father when they heard him calling.
Warrenby said, 'I did not call out. Perhaps the Imjim Quinkins
are trying to steal the children.'

People from the hunting party called out and said they
had seen Moonbi and Leealin heading towards Boonbalbee,
the Quinkins' home.

Warrenby said to Margara, 'Here are the tracks of the hunting
party. We will look about for the tracks of our children.'
They searched and searched but found nothing.

The two willy-wagtails sat and watched. After a long search Margara said, 'Now we are certain the Imjim are trying to steal our children. They have brushed away their tracks so we cannot follow. We must run to Boonbalbee to save them.'

Moonbi said, 'I thought I heard our father call again,
but I cannot see his tracks anywhere. It is very strange.'

Leealin looked fearfully around and said, 'I don't like this place, there might be Imjim about, let's go home.'

The children felt drawn toward the dark cave. They moved closer and closer, they could not stop themselves.
Leealin said, 'I can see awful red eyes, let's run away from here, Moonbi.'

Just then a huge rock rolled down the cliff face—
a Timara had kicked it. This broke the spell the Imjim
had cast over the two children and now they were able
to turn and run towards their camp.

Moonbi and Leealin ran towards their camp. The Imjim
Quinkins from the awful cave started to chase them, but
the Timara called up all his friends and a battle began.

The Quinkins fought all night—biting, scratching, kicking
and banging each other with sticks—there was an awful noise.
When dawn came they all crawled away to nurse their wounds
in dark caves or rock crevices.

Moonbi and Leealin met their mother and father.
Together they all ran home through the darkening
bush to the safety and warmth of their campfire.

Far behind them they could hear the fierce battle
and terrible screeching of the fighting Quinkins.

Safe at home the family sat around their fire to eat
roast emu and yams that had been cooked by Grandmother.

And before they went to sleep Moonbi and Leealin
promised that never again would they wander alone
near the Quinkin-haunted caves of Boonbalbee.